Contents

INTRO

Hello dear reader, I'm Mykova. Even though I'm a raccoon I'm a travel blogger, kinda.

I've been to many beautiful places around the world. I can share a story or two about my experiences with you.

Wherever I go, I always take my favorite books with puzzles as it's always a good idea to learn something new, and kill time during those boring flights and hours of waiting for connections. It's also super funny and helps me socialize (yeah, raccoons socialize too)!

In this book you will get travel suggestions (and practical content too) about one of the greatest cities on planet and will be able to flex your brains.

Across

2. Name of a known NY river. (6 letters)
3. ... State Building. (6 letters)
4. Name of a famous scientist, whos eyeballs are still stored in one of the banks of NY city. (6 letters)
7. World known brand name and a second name of a fashion designer born in New York. (8 letters)
10. Parade, usually takes place on St. Patrick's day in New York. (5 letters)
14. Big ..., nickname of NY. (5 letters)
15. Tall building. (10 letters)
17. Ice hockey team based in NY. (7 letters)
18. An abbreviation of the municipal department in New York. (4 letters)
19. 3rd popular language in NY.(7 letters)
20. Name of the district in NY named after its first settler (5 letters)
22. Animal, mentioned in a movie about the famous NY street, which is a home of NY Stock Exchange. (4 letters)
23. Central District of NY. (9 letters)
24. Bridge name. (8 letters)
28. It's not illegal to dress and walk like this in NY. (7 letters)
30. The second name of the Hollywood actor born in New York. (6 letters)
32. Animal, a statue of which in NY depicts capitalism. (4 letters)
33. Ocean in NY. (8 letters)
34. Mollusc, its shells once paved not only the road on the Pearl street in NY, but also many buildings. (6 letters)
35. Second name of a bloody tyrant, statue of whom you may find on the roof of one of the NY buildings. (5 letters)
36. A broad road in a town or city, typically having trees at regular intervals along its sides. (6 letters)
37. Company which published this book and provides Travel Assistant service. (10 letters)

Down

1. The 360-degree viewing platform and eatery located near the top of the newly-rebuilt center. (11 letters)
2. ... statue. Iconic National Monument. (7 letters)
6. A square named after NY magazine. (5 letters)
8. Federal ... . The central banking system based in NY. (7 letters)
9. Football team based in NY. (6 letters)
11. First name of NY born iconic rapper. (5 letters)
12. St. ... Cathedral. (7 letters)
13. Second name of an actress starred in an famous TV Show about NY. (8 letters)
16. A trade center in NY with one of the best observation decks. (11 letters)
20. Activity popular among nature lovers which is often done in NY. (11 letters)
21. Fountain name, in Jewesh it means "House of mercy". (8 letters)
25. Color of a motor vehicle licensed to transport passengers. (6 letters)
26. Name of the popular NY park. (7 letters)
27. New York is a home of the highest number of these wealthy people. (11 letters)
29. Roman goddess of Wisdom, its statue stands on the Battle Hill in NY. (7 letters)
31. A network of tracks with the trains, movement organization, and personnel required for its working. It takes at least 24h to run it all in NY. (6 letters)
32. Road and street name, which originally was named Heeren Straat, meaning «Gentlemen's Way» or «Gentlemen's Street». (5 letters)

Empire State Building

One of the most popular attractions is the Empire State Building. Built in 1931, the building has 102 floors and is 1,250 feet tall. It is currently the tallest tower in New York City and the 2nd tallest building in the United States. The building attracts nearly 4 million visitors a year, and since it was first built, over 100 million people have gone up to its observation decks. For this reason, in pre-Covid era, the queues to access its viewpoints were sometimes never-ending.

The Empire State Building has two observation decks, the first on the 86th floor, with 360° degree views of the city and the second on the 102nd floor. Going to the first observation deck costs US$ 42 (€ 34.80) and going to the second costs an extra US $30 (€24.80).

— Tickets:
Adults: US$ 36 (€ 29.80)
Children (ages 6 to 12): US $31 (€ 25.70)
Senior (over 62): US $35 (€ 29)
Free entry with the New York Pass.
Empire State Building Ticket US$ 45.73

— Schedule
Every day from 8am to 2am. The last lift to the observation decks is at 1:15 am.

— Transport
Subway: 34th Street/Penn Station (lines 1, 2, 3, A, C and E) or 34th St - Avenue of the Americas (lines B, D, F, N, Q and R).
Bus: lines M2, M3, M4 M5, M16 and M34.
Location: Fifth Avenue, between 33rd and 34th streets

Taxi cabs in New York are big, comfortable, clean and even have a screen where you can play whatever you like, including a GPS so that you can verify the taxi's route. Although the subway and buses are quite efficient, it is still useful to take one of the iconic New York cabs from time to time. You will find these famous yellow vehicles literally on every corner of the Big Apple. However, when it rains it is almost impossible to find one that is empty.

Fares

Contrary to popular opinion, taxi cabs in New York are not overly expensive. The average price of a standard journey in Manhattan is about $10. These are the general rates:

Minimum fare: US$ 2.50 (€ 2.10).

Stretch of 320 meters: US$ 0.50 (€ 0.40) (US$ 1.56 (€ 1.30) per kilometre).

An hour wait: US$ 30 (€ 24.80).

City taxes: US$ 0.50 (€ 0.40)

Night supplement (from 8 pm to 6 am): US$ 0.50 (€ 0.40).

Peak hour supplement (from 4 pm to 8 pm): US$ 1 (€ 0.80)

▬ Fares to the Airport

Here are some examples of fares to the different airports from Manhattan. These are total prices, including tolls, tips, and supplements, which are more expensive than for the journeys within the city (for example the rush hour is US$ 4.50 (€ 3.70)).

JFK: Between US$ 70 (€ 58) and US$ 80 (€ 66.30).

La Guardia: Between US$ 35 (€ 29) and US$ 45 (€ 37.30).

Newark: Between US$ 80 (€ 66.30) and US$ 100 (€ 82.90). In general, taxis in New York are affordable compared to other cities like San Francisco or Las Vegas.

▬ Travel tip

Although it is not mandatory, normally you tip the driver between 10% and 15%, or at least round up to the closest dollar.

New York's most famous symbol, the Statue of Liberty, also known as Liberty Enlightening the World, is found on Liberty Island. This iconic monument of 151 feet 1 inch from base to torch, located on an island in Upper New York Bay, can only be visited by ferry. To get to the boat visitors have to head to the dock in Battery Park in Downtown Manhattan.

Schedule

The only access to Liberty Island is by ferry. The first ferry departs at 9:30am. To come back to Manhattan, the last ferry leaves Liberty Island at 3:30pm.
Open every day of the year except on 25 December.

Price

The ferry price includes a visit to Liberty Island and Ellis Island.
Adults: US$ 18.50 (€ 15.40).
Children (ages 4 to 12): US$ 9 (€ 7.50).
Seniors (over 62): US$ 14 (€ 11.60).

Free with the New York Pass.

Statue of Liberty and Ellis Island Guided Tour US$ 50.75

Transport

Ferry from Battery Park. To get to the dock:
Subway: South Ferry (line 1), Whitehall St/South Ferry (lines R and W) or Bowling Green (lines 4 and 5).
Bus: lines M1, M6 and M15.

Location

Liberty island, southeast of Manhattan

The original series aired on HBO from 1998 to 2004, spanning 94 episodes during its six seasons. The show, which followed best friends living in New York City, earned 54 Emmy nominations (winning seven) and 24 Golden Globe nods (winning eight). The show also led to two box-office hit movies. 2008's Sex and the City grossed over $415 million worldwide. Despite being slammed by critics, 2010's Sex and the City 2 brought in $294 million worldwide. "Sex and the city" became a symbol of New York thanks to fantastic work of actors and all film crew.

Sarah Jessica Parker announced that an official Sex and the City revival is coming! Filming will begin in New York, in spring 2021. At the moment, it is planned to shoot 10 half-hour episodes. According to the rumours, In new series Samantha Jones will be replaced by 2 new heroines - an African American and an Asian. They report that they decided to make the show as racially diverse and colorful as New York itself.

◼ Central Park

Central Park is New York's largest urban park and one of the biggest in the world, with 843 acres. This park has artificial lakes, waterfalls, meadows and wooded areas. You will also find the Central Park Zoo, among other attractions in this greenspace of New York. Moreover, usually there are a number of events in Central Park that you can check out on the official website of NYC parks department:
https://www.nycgovparks.org

Besides being the city's primary green lungs, Central Park is a favourite spot for many New Yorkers, as it is perfect for sunbathing, going for walks, or doing any outdoor sports. It's recommended to walk or to rent a bike to enjoy the park.

There are lots of bike rental stores around Central Park that are not very expensive, or you can book a guided bike tour online.

— Schedule
From 6am to 1am.

Tickets

The entrance to the Park is free, although some parts like the Central Park zoo charge an admissions fee.

Transport

Subway: lines 5, 6, 7, A, B, C and D.
Bus: lines M1, M2, M3 M4 and M10.

Location

Between 5th and 8th Avenue and 59th Street and 110th Street

St Patrick's Cathedral

The Cathedral of St. Patrick is the largest Neo-Gothic-style Roman Catholic cathedral in the United States. It was dedicated to the Patron Saint of Ireland.
Although the construction of the cathedral began in 1858, works were stopped during the American Civil War and the temple wasn't completed until 1879. St. Patrick's Cathedral is built of brick clad in marble, with a very characteristic Neo-Gothic-Style, making it a very unique building, especially when compared to the architecture surrounding it.

Inside, the church has two impressive pipe organs, of 3,920 and 5,918 tubes and a sculpture of Pietà. Due to its location, the cathedral becomes an extremely interesting contrast compared to its neighboring skyscrapers. The cathedral is situated in the center of Manhattan, on Fifth Avenue, and is a definite must-see.

Schedule
Every day: from 6:30am to 8:45pm.

— Transport

Subway: Fifth Avenue, 53RD St, lines E and M; 47-50th St-Rockefeller Ctr, lines B, D, F and M.
Bus: Eden Quay, lines 49, 49A, 49B, 50, 54A, 56A, 65, 65B, 77 and 77A.

Location:

Fifth Avenue, between 50th and 51th street

Manhattan

Manhattan is New York's most famous borough and also its most visited. In fact, most people believe Manhattan to be a synonym of New York City. Manhattan is a long island bounded by the Hudson River (to the west), by the East River (to the east) and Harlem (to the north). It has a land area of 22.83 square miles (59.1 km²).

Districts of Manhattan

Lower Manhattan: Is the southernmost part of the island of Manhattan and the point where New York was founded. In this area you will find the business district and various governing bodies. The boundaries of Lower Manhattan go from the south of the island to 14th Street.

Midtown Manhattan: Runs from 14th Street to 59th Street (southern part of Central Park). Its most famous area, with the greatest amount of skyscrapers, begins on 33rd Street, where the legendary Empire State Building is.

Upper Manhattan: Upper Manhattan starts in Central Park and finishes in 96th Street. The western part also includes Columbia University and the Cathedral of Saint John the Divine.

Harlem: This area begins after Upper Manhattan and finishes on 155th Street. Its most famous street is 125th Street, where you will find the Apollo Theatre.

Washington Heights: This area is found in the northern part of the island (220th Street). It is named after Fort Washington, a fort built during the eighteenth century to protect the area from the British.

— Top Attractions in Manhattan

Ninety percent of the most popular attractions are found in Manhattan and on the island. All the life of the borough is concentrated in the area known as Midtown, north of 31st Street. In Manhattan, you will find the unequaled Empire State Building, the Rockefeller Center, the surprising Chrysler Building, the fascinating Times Square, the controversial MoMA, and other top attractions.

Lower Manhattan was as important in the past as it is presently. In this area you will find Wall Street and the financial district that determines the world's economy.

To experience the «other Manhattan» visit the north Manhattan district of Harlem.

You may or may not be aware of this fact, but when Albert Einstein died in 1955 his brain was removed to be studied. Approximately 20 years later it would be "rediscovered", studied some more and then would be returned to Einstein's granddaughter Evelyn. All in all one could say it makes a fun story and a semi-accomplishment for science. Dr. Harvey sectioned the preserved brain into 170 pieces in a lab at the University of Pennsylvania, but he did not have permission or a legal right to remove and keep the brain for himself. Harvey didn't only take the brain, but he also removed Einstein's eyeballs and gave them to Henry Abrams; Einstein's eye doctor. They remain to this day in a safe deposit box in New York City. Exact location is not known, but you can try to find it out.

Hudson River

The Hudson originates in several small postglacial lakes in the Adirondack Mountains near Mount Marcy, the highest point in New York, and flows about 315 miles (507 km) through the eastern part of the state. City officials are calling the Hudson's water quality the best it has been in a century. Parks department officials don't advise to swim in the Hudson, which has strong currents, no lifeguards and few access points.

National Geographic Traveler named the Hudson Valley one of the top 20 must-see destinations in the world. It is hard to disagree with this opinion, because this place has what to offer for all tastes. Among its entertainments are argiculture tourism, arts and culture museums and theaters, restaurants, historic buildings, recreational outdoor activities and many more.

The Federal Reserve

The Federal Reserve NY is one of the world's most powerful banks. It is located in the Financial District of Manhattan and is one of the 12 regional Reserve Banks of the Federal Reserve System aka «The Fed».

Visitors may tour the bank's underground vault, purportedly the largest gold repository in the world, and study more than 800 coins and medals from the American Numismatic Society. All tours, as well as admission to this NYC bank are free. However, reservations are required. MAX 30 people are allowed to tour the New York Fed Bank at the same time.

Address:
33 Liberty Street New York, US

Hours
Mon.-Fri. 10am-3pm

Schedule
Mondays. Closed on all bank holidays.

This ebook from Boxedtrips is provided with FREE Travel Assistant service for 3 hours for your trip planning or during your actual trip.

Travel Assistant service includes the following tasks (but not limited to):
– search for any tickets, search for the restaurants and booking tables
– search for hotels, apartments as per your preferences
– building custom itineraries within the city, from the desired location
– booking transfers, calling taxi
– researching activities for kids
– booking tours
and any other reasonable requests are provided at no cost. Any other service requests are provided at additional cost, which is always confirmed in advance.
Request your Travel Assistant using contact details below.

We would love to hear your feedback about the book and your trip!

For all inquiries regarding this guide please contact us at assist@boxedtrips.com
or via any messengers WhatsApp/Viber/Telegram +380634356439

Instagram
https://www.instagram.com/boxedtrips/

Facebook
https://www.facebook.com/boxedtripss/

You may request custom travel plan for any city at
http://boxedtrips.com